Gardening in
Ornamental Containers

Gardening in Ornamental Containers

THE ROYAL HORTICULTURAL SOCIETY

Cassell Educational Limited
Villiers House, 41/47 Strand
London WC2N 5JE
for the Royal Horticultural Society

First published 1987
Second impression 1988
Third impression 1989
Second edition 1991

British Library Cataloguing in Publication Data
Waite, Ray
  Gardening in ornamental containers. — (A Wisley
  handbook)
  1. Container gardening
  I. Title   II. Royal Horticultural Society
  III. Series
  635.9′86   SB418

  ISBN 0-304-32005-6

Photographs by Michael Warren, The Harry Smith
Collection and John Garey
Typeset by Chapterhouse Ltd, Formby
Printed in Hong Kong by Wing King Tong Co. Ltd.

Cover: a concrete urn with basketwork decoration filled
with pelargoniums, dark blue lobelia and candytuft.
  Photograph by S. & O. Mathews
p.1: hot colours in terracotta — rudbeckia, tagetes and
Helichrysum petiolare 'Limelight'.
p.2: a hanging basket overflowing with trailing and upright
fuchsias, pelargoniums and a touch of pale yellow provided
by petunias.
Back cover: Cannas and the glaucous foliage of *Melianthus
major* surround an urn of *Cordyline australis, Fuchsia
magellanica* 'Versicolor' and purple petunias.
  Photographs by Andrew Lawson

Contents

Impatiens planted on its own in an elegant terracotta pot which has been positioned with care
Opposite: an old farm cart transformed into an eye-catching container

Introduction

Vases, urns, troughs and other ornamental pots have been an important part of gardens for hundreds of years, often enhancing the overall effect in their own right. But never before has container gardening been practised on such a large scale as it is today. Permanent plantings of trees, shrubs and conifers in purpose-built receptacles have become a feature of our town and city centres, while tubs and troughs of seasonal bedding decorate traffic islands and paved public areas. The modern domestic garden, ever shrinking in size, is invariably transformed into a patio and furnished with all sorts of plants in containers. Even people without gardens can resort to window boxes and hanging baskets for a colourful display and these are increasingly popular. Indoors, of course, container gardening is widespread and house plants abound in offices, foyers, waiting rooms and homes.

This book is intended to show what can be achieved by 'gardening without a garden'—using containers outside. It describes the various types of container available, including the conventional ones and the more unusual or unexpected, and also suggests do-it-yourself ideas for constructing containers cheaply. General advice is given on cultivation and propagation. This is followed by a list of recommended plants for both seasonal and permanent schemes, with details of their flowering times, hardiness, special needs and suitability for particular situations.

Conventional types of container

VASES, URNS, POTS AND JARDINIERES

Traditional natural materials like stone and clay will give the most pleasing effect, although the modern alternatives of plastic and glass fibre can be very acceptable if treated sympathetically. There is a wide range of styles and sizes available, at different prices. When choosing a container, one should ensure it matches or associates well with its surroundings, especially paving and walling, and one often finds that a vase or urn with simple lines will fit in best.

Always check that the container has sufficient room for planting and a reasonable depth for the growing medium, especially at the edges, as excessive drying out can be a problem. A minimum depth of 4 inches (10cm) at the edges is recommended. It is also wiser to avoid a container with a narrow mouth, because this gives little width at the rim and can be difficult to plant.

Provision for drainage is important and there should be one good-sized hole, or several, in the base. A large hole will need covering with a piece of old clay flower pot, concave side downwards. For smaller holes, broken brick or stones will allow for free drainage. It is a good idea to raise the container on bricks or blocks so that the water can run away, but make sure that it is stable.

Terracotta containers, except the frost-resistant types, may be damaged by frost in winter and should be kept dry and under cover. Even the dry shelter of a hedge or evergreen tree gives good protection and, if the containers can be emptied first, so much the better.

TROUGHS, TUBS AND IMPROVISED PLANTERS

These containers are made from similar materials and some of the plastic and glass fibre models are extremely good. Wood also plays a part and lead is used by at least one manufacturer who has faithfully copied the design and finish of traditional containers. It is still possible to find specialist craftsmen working with metal.

Properly coopered wooden half-barrels or tubs are becoming more difficult to obtain and are quite expensive. If they are to be stored for any length of time, it is worth keeping them wet. This swells the wood and prevents individual slats falling apart. The interior should be charred to reduce rotting, a blow-lamp being the easiest method of doing this. Unseasoned wood should be treated with preservative, using only products recommended for applying to wooden greenhouses and avoiding those like creosote which would harm the plants.

Large planters may be constructed from railway sleepers, fixed together by long coach bolts or large staples at the corners. They can be made to suit a particular space and tiered to give different levels of planting. Beware of splinters and tar. Obviously, all sorts of troughs can be made from wood and painted to match the exterior decoration of the building or other surroundings. Rough sawn wood may be covered in cork bark, which is very weather-resistant.

Bricks, manufactured walling, concrete blocks or stone can be converted into good solid planters. Stone may be made up without cement and sand bonding so that the container can be easily moved or extended as the season or your mood dictates. In this way the gardener can experiment with positioning and size before making a final decision.

Plastic containers can be improvised from various tubs, such as those used to hold putty, and are ideal for small areas. Drainage holes should be made in the bottom and the outside can be painted with 'Snowcem' to give a rough stone-like finish.

WINDOW BOXES

Window boxes are generally used in sunny positions and planted for seasonal display. However, they can also be adapted to permanent planting or, with a suitable range of plants, they can even be placed in quite shady situations. It is interesting to note that the special climate of London, produced by the warmth of the buildings, allows reasonably tender plants to flourish in window boxes and it is not uncommon to see cinerarias, poinsettias, *Solanum capsicastrum* and pot chrysanthemums growing in the open air in winter. Plants of this sort are best plunged in peat in their pots.

Because of their exposed position, window boxes are particularly prone to rapid drying out and watering should always be carried out early and thoroughly. Like other containers, they will need drainage holes, which can be conveniently made in the base at the rear edge. Don't forget that some water is bound to splash down, so be careful about siting anything underneath. (For further notes on watering, see p. 22.)

Proprietary plastic liners are obtainable which help to over-

Above: a variegated hosta in a half-barrel is skilfully repeated in the border beyond and is ideal for a shady situation

Below: a most unexpected receptacle successfully planted with impatiens to demonstrate the many possibilities of container gardening

come the drying problem, or one can cut polythene sheeting to size and lay it inside the box before filling up with potting compost. Several slits should be cut in the bottom of the lining to allow excess water to drain away. Such linings will also prolong the life of wooden window boxes.

It is important to fix window boxes securely. Even the lighter peat-based composts can become quite heavy, especially when saturated with water. One or two brackets underneath the box, secured to the wall with strong screws, provide the most effective support.

The size of window box will inevitably be dictated by the situation, but it is wise to choose as large a one as possible. Generous planting will result in a better display than a single row of plants, while a larger amount of compost will dry out less quickly and allow for better root growth. With larger boxes it is often more convenient to have separate planting units or sections, which will be easy to handle and fairly light to lift if made from wire mesh and lined with polythene. These also enable one to establish the plants in advance and place them in position when in flower.

WALL POTS AND HAY MANGERS

Somewhat akin to window boxes in their effect, both these types of container are widely available.

Clay wall pots are usually designed to be hooked onto a wall and tend to be quite small, roughly equal in size to a 5- or 6-inch (12.5–15cm) pot. They are best devoted to one kind of plant and are particularly effective if several pots are grouped together. However, they may dry out very quickly, especially when exposed to full sun and wind.

Wall pots arranged in a vertical line can be very attractive, but be careful when watering not to let drips damage the flowers in the lower containers. Ideally, the pots should be put on the ground for watering and, once they have drained through, returned to the wall. Plastic wall pots are also obtainable, many of them fitted with a water reservoir.

Genuine hay mangers can still be found in antique shops and at auctions and an enterprising blacksmith will often make one up to order. Their size and scale should be considered in relation to the wall space and also to the setting. In modern surroundings, for instance, the effect could be quite incongruous.

A piece of large meshed chicken netting should be attached to the bars of the manger to hold in the compost. The netting in turn is lined with moss, followed by a sheet of polythene which will help conserve moisutre. Sphagnum moss is the best, but is increasingly difficult and expensive to buy. Moreover, it is becoming much less abundant in the wild and every effort should be made to conserve it. Black plastic sheeting on its own is satisfactory, although it looks rather unattractive, especially in the early stages before the plants have grown enough to hide it. Green polythene is not much better.

HANGING BASKETS

Hanging baskets have become extremely popular in recent years. Although traditional wire baskets are still common, the solid plastic kinds are increasingly preferred. These are easy to plant and maintain and often have a water reservoir incorporated, either a saucer clipped on to the basket or as an internal fitment. The hooks and hangers are usually made from plastic and the whole unit is therefore very durable. With their flat bases, these plastic baskets are convenient to work on and can be stood on the greenhouse staging or floor while plants are being established in the early stages. At present they are generally available only in small sizes, but are very effective when planted with a single type of plant.

Wire baskets, on the other hand, can be obtained in various dimensions, some with a galvanized finish and others with a plastic coating. The larger ones, of course, may be planted with an assortment of plants. Being proportionately heavier, they will require stronger brackets or other means of support.

The usual method of planting is to line the basket with moss to retain the potting compost. An additional layer of plastic sheeting can be placed inside the moss to reduce drying out. The basket should be stood on a flower pot of suitable size to keep it upright and steady while planting.

One advantage of a wire basket is that plants can be grown through the sides between the metal strands, which gives a splendid overall display. In this case, it is not practical to include the polythene, since the moss and compost have to be built up in stages. A small amount of moss should be placed in the bottom and covered with a layer of potting compost, in which the first batch of plants is planted round the edge by carefully pushing the root balls between the wires. The roots are then covered with compost, more moss is added at the sides, together with another layer of compost, and the process is repeated until the basket is filled. There should be plenty of moss at the top to make a rim which will retain water and prevent any compost being washed over the edge.

There are several brands of basket liner which can be purchased and used instead of moss. One sort made of foam plastic is particularly good. It is a flat disc in which slits are cut from the perimeter towards the centre, thus allowing it to be moulded to the shape of the basket. The plant roots are then gently squeezed through the vertical gaps.

Similar liners are also made from strong impregnated cardboard or compressed fibre. Holes may be cut in the sides with an old apple corer or other tool so that the root systems can be pushed through.

Square wooden baskets, consisting of small slats of a durable wood such as teak, are still in common use for growing certain greenhouse orchids and tree-dwelling plants.

A decorative wooden hanging basket with ivy-leaf pelargonium and the delightful trailing bellflower *Campanula isophylla*

Unusual containers

The gardener's ingenuity can be a great asset when it comes to finding or making containers and virtually anything that will hold compost and has some provision for drainage can be adapted.

WHEELBARROWS

Wooden wheelbarrows make large containers which are especially suitable for seasonal bedding and those with wooden or well-disguised metal wheels always seem to look best. Traditionally, English elm is the timber employed in the main part of the barrow, being long lasting even when saturated with water. Other woods should be treated with a preservative, if a natural colour is preferred, or may be painted. There are also smaller, less robust wheelbarrows on the market.

HOLLOW LOGS

These make attractive containers and once again elm is the most durable wood for the purpose. Large diameter sections cut in lengths of about 1 foot (30cm) give an ample planting depth for most plants. Any rotting wood should be removed and the inside cleaned back to the solid wood, which is then charred in the same way as a tub (see p. 9). Logs can be arranged at different heights to create a pleasing group.

CHIMNEY POTS

Clay chimney pots vary in size, design and colour and can be an effective feature on a patio or terrace. Although becoming difficult to find, and therefore expensive, they are well worth searching for in builders' yards and on demolition sites. Their small diameter can be a disadvantage, limiting the choice of plants, and a group of at least three pots may give a better display. Large glazed or unglazed drainpipes can be used in the same way.

Chimney pots or pipes should be partly filled with pebbles, gravel or builders' ballast. They can be lined with polythene, with holes cut in the bottom, to reduce drying out.

Left: a small wooden wheelbarrow painted to match its surroundings and burgeoning with African and French marigolds
Right: an old tree stump hollowed out and planted with zonal pelargonium and *Calocephalus brownii*, together with lobelia and ivy at the side and base

SHELLS

Although they might seem rather alien to the modern garden, large clam-type shells were very much in vogue during Victorian times and earlier. When grottoes were fashionable, shells were used either as decoration or more functionally in association with a cascade of water. They can provide an interesting container for small plants, such as pansies, polyanthus and primroses for spring flowering, followed by *Impatiens* and *Mimulus* in summer. Drainage is difficult because it is almost impossible to drill holes, but if the shell is tilted foward slightly, much of the excess water collected will seep out.

SINKS

Stone sinks, also from bygone days, are ideal for small alpines. One can achieve complete planting schems in miniature and grow a wide selection of plant gems in a group of sinks.

Above: cool colours in an elegant handmade terracotta pot; white argyranthemums and petunias combine with verbenas and *Helichrysum petiolare*

Below: a litter bin completely covered with *Begonia semperflorens*—an effective use of an otherwise ugly container

A modern glazed sink can also be treated to make an extremely good hewn stone imitation. After removing any pieces of waste pipe left behind, the exterior glazing should be scored to give a key for the initial coating of adhesive. To this is applied the imitation stone covering called hypertufa, made up of equal parts of peat, builder's sand and cement, which should be kneaded on to the outside, over the rim and down the inside, so that there will be no gap between it and the compost.

The work is best carried out in the autumn to allow a longer period for drying and thus ensure a stronger bond. The sink should be kept in a frost-free place during the process. Once the surfaces have dried, they may be painted two or three times with liquid fertilizer, to produce a more natural appearance and hasten the growth of moss. (See also the Wisley handbook on alpines.)

CAR TYRES

Unlikely as it may seem, rubber car tyres can be transformed into containers which are perfectly acceptable when covered with plant growth. Painted with plastic emulsion paint (PEP), they can be used singly or stacked on top of each other to give a suitable depth of compost. Plants should be placed between the tyres as they are stacked and the compost filled in around the root. The tyres will have a long and useful life, although obviously they will not be easy to move once planted.

LITTER BASKETS

Wire litter baskets of the type seen in car parks have great potential. Taller baskets 3 feet (1m) or more high can be used as a free-standing feature, while the smaller waste-paper kind may be turned into a large hanging basket. Alternatively, one can make a cylindrical basket by driving thin stakes into the ground or fixing them to a base and securing chicken netting to them. In this way the diameter and height can be chosen to suit the situation.

Taller containers may need to be stabilized by means of a pipe or stake, which is driven down the centre and into the ground underneath. In addition, a piece of plastic pipe should be inserted in the centre of the basket. It is cut to roughly two thirds the depth of the container, with a few holes bored in the bottom half, allowing more even penetration when filled with water. A lining of moss will retain the compost in the same way as for a hanging basket. Plants can then be grown round the sides to achieve a massed pillar effect.

Containers for special purposes

STRAWBERRY POTS

A strawberry pot made of clay is a most attractive container, best described as a large jar with holes in the sides. Each hole is of sufficient size to take a strawberry root system and is made with a cupped lower lip to retain compost and water. Once filled with compost, these pots become very heavy and somewhat unwieldy so are best planted up *in situ*. They are now quite expensive, especially those made of frost-resistant clay, but can look very charming, especially when used for flowering plants such as busy lizzies and fibrous-rooted begonias.

A tower of plastic strawberry pots planted with impatiens and, perhaps inadvisedly, topped with pansies

There are also smaller versions for growing herbs. Thyme, marjoram and hyssop are ideal and can be planted together in one pot. Parsley pots are based on the same principle.

Two kinds of plastic strawberry planter are on the market. One is quite large and mounted on a small wooden platform fitted with castors, which allows the container to be turned so that all the developing plants and fruit have a share of direct sunlight. (The idea can be similarly adapted for clay pots.) It is possible to make a large planter from a plastic dustbin with holes cut in the sides, or a strong polythene bag. All these sizeable containers need a length of perforated pipe or a core of chicken netting inserted down the centre for watering purposes.

The other type of planter commonly available is much smaller in diameter and comprises a tower made up of sections with cupped holes.

BULB POTS AND BOWLS

Bulb pots of clay or plastic are shaped like miniature squat Ali Baba jars with holes in the sides. The bulbs are placed inside the holes and held in position as the pot is filled with compost. Crocuses are particularly effective when grown in them and grape hyacinths and scillas can also be recommended.

Bulb bowls do not have drainage holes and it is therefore important to use bulb fibre or a similar very open growing medium.

Both these types of container are more often seen indoors, but they can be used quite successfully outside.

GROWING BAGS

The concept of growing bags is totally different to that of all the containers previously discussed, but they merit a mention here because of their importance and popularity. The plastic bags containing the compost tend to be rather garish in colour and, while this does not matter in a greenhouse, they may be somewhat conspicuous in a conservatory or on a patio. Canes pushed into the compost require firm support, which can be achieved by an overhead wire or, where this is not possible or desirable, by a proprietary framework fixing the canes securely at the base.

Growing bags are deservedly popular for several reasons. They contain a sterile and consistent compost which is easy to handle; they can be used in many situations and make the annual preparation, replacement or sterilization of greenhouse borders unnecessary; and they can take a primary crop such as tomatoes, followed

A growing bag newly planted with bedding plants—a practical if not the most decorative container

by a secondary crop like winter lettuce, after which the compost can be used in the garden as a source of humus. Many gardeners find the mini-size growing bags especially convenient.

RING CULTURE POTS

This system, traditionally applied to growing tomatoes, has been largely superseded by the more convenient growing bag, but some gardeners still prefer it. In brief, the method consists of standing a bottomless cardboard pot on clean ash, sand or ballast and filling it with compost. The roots grow through the bottom of the pot into the lower layer, which is kept well watered, and liquid feed is applied directly to the growing medium in the container.

SELF-WATERING CONTAINERS

Now widely used for indoor display, self-watering containers can also be used outside. They are helpful when plants are likely to be left unattended for any length of time, although they are relatively expensive. They come in various shapes, sizes and finishes. The basic principle is that the planter is fitted with a reservoir from which the water rises to the compost above by means of wicks. A small float is connected to a marker at the top of the rim and indicates the amount of water in reserve.

Management and maintenance

THE GROWING MEDIUM

The kind of growing medium required will depend very much on the plant and its situation.

For permanent planting out of doors, plants will do best in a loam-based compost. Good drainage is essential and can be provided by filling the base of the container to a depth of several inches with broken brick, old rubble, large stones etc. Ideally, chopped-up turf should be placed on top of the drainage material before adding the compost, but coarse peat sievings or well-rotted manure are an acceptable alternative. Containers should be filled to the brim with compost and well firmed during the process, allowing some space at the top for watering.

Some settling of the compost is inevitable in the first year, but try to prevent excessive sinking as this looks ugly and deprives the roots of compost. If possible, large containers should be filled well before planting to allow the compost to settle first.

The John Innes formula is still the best for a loam-based compost. JI no. 3 mixture, which contains more fertilizer than JI no. 2, is recommended for vigorous plants. It may be bought ready-made or alternatively prepared at home, by mixing 7 parts by volume of sterilised loam with 3 parts of peat and 2 parts of grit or coarse sand (be sure to use coarse sand and not the finer type), to which is added a balanced fertilizer to keep the plants growing for several weeks. An increased amount of loam will be beneficial for larger containers in which trees and shrubs are to be established.

When a lighter compost is required, for example in hanging baskets or window boxes, a peat-based kind should be chosen. There are many commercial brands available, but for gardeners who wish to mix their own a good general formula is 3 parts by volume of moss peat to one part of coarse sand, with a base fertilizer added in quantities recommended by the manufacturer. Proprietary peat-based composts contain less nutrients and will therefore need feeding sooner.

Always remember to soak peat thoroughly before mixing. Once it has dried out completely (for example on the shelf in a garden centre), it can be difficult to wet properly again. For this reason, some ready-mixed composts contain a wetting agent to facilitate the process. It is also important to ensure that containers do not

Clematis macropetala 'Maidwell Hall' in a wine jar, a good example of permanent planting in a large container

dry out when planted up with a peat-based compost. In fact, both loam and peat-based composts benefit from the incorporation of water-retentive polymer granules. These are capable of absorbing and then releasing a large amount of moisture over a long period, at the same time maintaining a good free-draining physical structure to the compost.

WATERING

Lack of water is probably the commonest explanation for disappointing results when growing plants in containers. Hanging baskets, wall pots, window boxes, free-standing urns and vases are all particularly vulnerable, especially in hot weather, and may need watering at least once a day. A light breeze can cause serious drying out even in dull weather and, in a densely planted container, water will simply run off the leaves without soaking the compost after a downpour of rain. Self-watering containers fitted with a small reservoir are obviously helpful, but they are not equipped to keep the compost moist for any length of time.

Planters, window boxes and growing bags can be fitted with irrigation lines. Basically, water comes from nozzles placed at strategic points along a length of tubing which leads back to the water source. The number of nozzles will depend on the size of container and the amount of water required to thoroughly moisten the compost. At the height of sophistication, watering can be automated, although most gardeners will be content to turn on a tap.

Hanging baskets are often difficult to water and a hose may be useful for the purpose. A recent innovation is a hand-held bottle which pumps water up a short lance with a bent top. It is simple and efficient but only satisfactory for dealing with a small number of hanging baskets.

FEEDING

It is not always appreciated that container plants require supplementary feeding and that the compost alone cannot provide sufficient nutrients to maintain good growth after the first two or three weeks. This applies even to containers planted for seasonal display and all the more to long-term planting schemes. One of the simplest methods of feeding is liquid fertilizer, which is easily applied and in a form readily assimilated by the plants. Overall, a mixed fertilizer containing all the essential elements will be the best choice, although a fertilizer with a higher nitrogen content will prove necessary to boost growth and thus prolong flowering.

An alternative is to sprinkle a dry fertilizer on the surface. The resin-coated slow-release type is particularly useful for hanging baskets, while perennial woody plants will benefit from an annual dressing of a general fertilizer.

PROTECTION FROM FROST

Where containers are very close to buildings, they are usually sufficiently protected by the latent heat of the walls and one or two degrees of air frost in late spring will do little harm. However, it is safer to wait until May or June before planting up containers with half-hardy bedding plants. If a late frost is expected, plants can be covered with sheets of newspaper.

In the autumn, it is a wise precaution to take propagating material of tender plants before the threat of severe frosts. A further advantage is that cuttings tend to root quickly in September and the resulting plants will be able to become established for overwintering in a frost-free greenhouse.

In exposed positions, vulnerable subjects such as bay trees

should be moved to a more sheltered part of the garden or placed in a cold greenhouse.

If extra protection is required, hessian or bracken can be used. Both may be supported by means of bamboo canes and kept in place by covering with wire or plastic netting.

PROPAGATION

Seeds

Half-hardy annuals are generally raised from seed sown in heat in February and March. A temperature of about 70° (21°C) suits most of them and after germination the seedlings can be grown on in a cooler temperature of 50 to 60°F (10–16°C). When large enough to handle, they should be pricked out into bigger trays or singly into pots to allow room for development. They should not be planted out until the risk of frost has passed, which may be April or May depending on area. They will require hardening off first to acclimatize them to outdoor conditions and should be moved to a frame or cloche, or placed outside initially for a few hours each day and then for longer periods.

Cuttings

Softwood cuttings are leafy shoots usually taken in the spring when growth is active; semi-hardwood cuttings are riper stems taken later in the season. In both cases they will need some sort of protection, such as a propagating case or frame, to prevent wilting. It is important to select good healthy material from non-flowering growths whenever possible.

September is the best month for autumn propagation and allows the cuttings to become well rooted and established in their pots before the onset of winter. They should be protected from frost.

Silver-foliaged plants should be kept on the dry side, especially when temperatures are low.

Above: containers grouped on a patio, with pelargonium, impatiens, French marigold, cineraria and a standard fuchsia, and two impressive urns
Below: half-hardy summer bedding plants—heliotrope, verbena, chrysanthemum, ivy-leaf pelargonium, sweet alyssum—used to good effect

Plants for outside containers

The range of plants suitable for growing in containers is enormous, extending far beyond the familiar geraniums, fuchsias and lobelias. Apart from one's own personal preferences, there are many factors dictating the choice of plants.

The most important consideration is the basic nature of the site, whether it is sunny or shaded, sheltered or exposed, which way the walls face and how much space is at one's disposal.

Then, you should think about the type of container for which the plants are destined. Would it look better with a mixture of plants, or a single kind, or just one specimen? What will be the ultimate effect using, say, trailing or bushy plants? And will the plants or the container itself be the main feature?

The actual requirements of the plants are, of course, a priority. Some of the most popular annuals, for instance, need a sunny spot to perform well; and shrubs should be grown in containers which afford plenty of room for their roots. The availability of a greenhouse or some sort of winter protection broadens your scope so that you can include half-hardy and tender plants and also increase stock at home.

In the end, it is a question of the amount of time and money you are prepared to devote to growing plants in containers. If you regard container gardening as a means of achieving a colourful show in the summer, as many people do, you will find it quite labour-intensive. Bedding plants will have to be bought in or raised from seed, and once planted in their containers, will demand constant attention—watering, feeding, deadheading and so on. On the other hand, if you invest in more permanent plants like shrubs and perennials, the initial expense may be greater but the day-to-day maintenance will be less and the results can be enjoyed for several years.

Perhaps the best form of container gardening is a combination of the two approaches, the temporary and the long-term, in which plants are selected both for the seasonal interest of their flowers and for the more lasting contribution of their foliage and shape.

The following list is by no means exhaustive, but gives suggestions for plants that are particularly recommended for growing in containers outside. It includes annuals, perennials and shrubs, arranged under their botanical names in alphabetical order. These are followed by general entries on alpines, bulbs, conifers, vegetables, herbs and fruit, starting on p. 57.

ABUTILON

A. × *hybridum* is a tender shrub with chalice-shaped, mallow flowers in shades of orange, salmon or maroon, which appear in early summer and continue right through to the autumn months. It is easily raised from seed from an early March sowing under glass. Cuttings can also be taken to reproduce particular colours, overwintered in frost-free conditions and grown on the following year. It is best used as an accent plant in tubs, urns and planters, as is the heavily variegated form 'Savitzii'. This must be propagated by cuttings and is not hardy.

A. striatum 'Thompsonii' is probably the most popular of all yellow variegated pot plants, further enhanced by its orange flowers. It is capable of making quite large plants fairly quickly and is worth propagating annually by means of cuttings. Although withstanding slight early autumn frosts, it requires winter protection in a frost-free place.

An abutilon lends emphasis to a rich medley of plants, including a bright red verbena, in this handsome urn

AGAPANTHUS

There are many good hybrids of this plant, which is related to the lily. It is particularly fine on its own in large vases or tubs, where its flowers of white or shades of blue above the striking strap-shaped leaves will make a bold display on patios and terraces in late summer and autumn. Although numerous hardy hybrids exist, they cannot be regarded as such when grown in containers, as their roots become vulnerable to extreme cold. They therefore require winter protection. They are increased by division in the spring.

AGAVE AMERICANA

This succulent perennial is another plant needing winter protection. Its stiff rosette of spiny leaves has a sub-tropical air and the yellow- or white-margined forms, *A. americana* var. *marginata*, are particularly effective. The many suckers provide material for easy propagation. They should be removed with a sharp knife and potted singly in small pots, using a sandy compost, in autumn or spring.

AGERATUM HOUSTONIANUM

This very popular annual bedding plant may be raised from seed sown in gentle heat in March. 'Adriatic', 'Blue Blazer' and 'Blue Mink' are all good for edging containers, together with the white forms 'Spindrift' and 'White Cushion'. The taller-growing cultivars 'Blue Bouquet' and 'Tall Blue' mix well with other plants.

The delightful chrysanthemum 'Jamaica Primrose' with petunias, geraniums, mimulus and helichrysum

ANTIRRHINUM MAJUS

The ever-popular **snapdragons** are usually grown as annuals and always give a cheerful show, although they are really only suitable for large containers. They can be sown in January and February in gentle heat and then pricked out and hardened off for planting out in their flowering positions. They may be planted even before the risk of frost has passed. A very wide range of colours and heights is available, some reaching at least 3 feet (1m) tall, the dwarf ones hardly exceeding 6 inches (15cm). Where antirrhinum rust is prevalent, a few rust-resistant cultivars of medium height can be obtained, although their resistance may not last the whole season.

ARABIS

The pink and white forms of A. *alpina* make good carpeting plants and are easily raised from seed, sown in spring under glass or out of doors in early summer.

A. *blepharophylla* 'Spring Charm' is very compact and has carmine flowers.

ARGYRANTHEMUM

A. *frutescens* (Chrysanthemum *frutescens*), the **Paris daisy** or **marguerite** as it is often known, is widely used in hanging baskets and also in tubs, vases and urns. It can be trained as a standard and underplanted for the summer. It is half-hardy and should be propagated annually in autumn or spring by softwood cuttings. The type with white daisy flowers is most familiar, but there are one or two with cushion-centred pink flowers and feathery grey-green leaves.

A. *leucanthemum* is a hardy perennial with dense yellow flowers, while the cultivar 'Jamaica Primrose' is a paler yellow.

A. *foeniculaceum* is a shrubby **chrysanthemum** with glaucous, much-divided leaves, best grown for foliage effect. (See p. 32.)

ARTEMISIA

A. 'Powis Castle' is a splendid silver foliage plant which can be hardy in favoured positions. However, it is safer to raise new plants each year in autumn from semi-hardwood cuttings and keep them in a frost-free place through the winter.

29

ARUNDINARIA VIRIDISTRIATA

This dwarf **bamboo** has leaves of dark green striped with yellow. It is a most attractive variegated plant, seen at its best in late summer. It is hardy and may be propagated by careful division of the roots in late spring or early autumn.

AUBRIETA DELTOIDEA

Usually seen as a rock plant, this perennial does equally well as an underplanting for spring bulbs. Pink, mauve and blue shades are dominant. It may be propagated by division, cuttings or seed.

BEGONIA

B. pendula is a superb plant for hanging baskets. It requires warmth (75°F; 23°C) to raise from seed, but if tubers are obtained they can be started into growth in the spring in frost-free conditions. There are red, pink and orange cultivars, all giving a good display throughout the summer. The tuberous begonias are excellent for troughs and planters, especially the Non-Stop F_1 hybrids. Propagated from seed sown in heat during early spring, the tubers may be stored over winter and brought into growth again by placing in a seed tray containing peat and keeping in a warm greenhouse or frame.

B. semperflorens, the fibrous-rooted begonia, is deservedly popular. It has a long flowering season and comes in a range of colours from white through pink to red, some cultivars even having bronze leaves. It needs warmth to raise from seed, but most nurserymen have plants available. Advances are continually being made in breeding. The following are particularly recommended for tubs, troughs, window boxes and hanging baskets—'Frilly Pink', 'Frilly Red', 'Pink Avalanche'. (See p. 16.)

None of the bedding begonias are hardy.

BELLIS PERENNIS

The common **daisy** has produced many cultivated forms, large- and small- and double-flowered, in white, pink and red. They flower in spring and summer and, although perennial, are best treated as biennials. They should be sown in boxes or direct into a frame and then either pricked off into boxes or planted out in a nursery plot before moving to their flowering positions in autumn.

BERBERIS

The **barberries**, characterised by their spring growth and yellow flowers in spring, include several useful evergreen shrubs for permanent planting in larger containers. 'Nana', a cultivar of *B. buxifolia*, makes a dense, low mound, while *B. candidula* is a slightly larger dome-shaped bush with bright yellow flowers. 'Irwinii' and 'Corallina Compacta' are two dwarf forms of *B. × stenophylla*.

BRUGMANSIA ARBOREA

This shrub can be raised from seed, although normally grown from cuttings, and ultimately makes a large plant some 5 feet (1.5m) or more tall and as wide. Its huge, white, hanging trumpets are very fragrant and give a fine summer display. Plants must be protected from frost and should be cut back hard each spring, shortening the previous year's growth to two buds. It is ideal for a sunny position outside, in a fairly large container. (See p. 32.)

CALCEOLARIA RUGOSA 'SUNSHINE'

This half-hardy plant is happy in sun or light shade and flowers throughout the summer from an early spring sowing under glass. The inflated flower pouches are clear yellow and held on long stems.

CALOCEPHALUS BROWNII

This is a tender shrub of wiry growth covered with dense, white, woolly hairs. Its overall silver appearance and non-rampant growth make it a good filler plant. It should be propagated by cuttings in the autumn. (See p. 15.)

CAMELLIA

The many cultivars of *C. japonica*, one of the hardiest species, are excellent in tubs and pots, except in the north and Scotland where they do not succeed. The *C. × williamsii* varieties are perhaps even better as they tend to be more free-flowering, although more open in habit, and will flower well in the north. The numerous hybrids of *C. reticulata* are also ideal if protected from frost.

Camellias do very well in town gardens and, with their handsome, evergreen, glossy leaves, are attractive even when not in

Above: a superb arrangement of containers and statues on a terrace, dominated by the double form of *Brugmansia arborea* and a stately white lily

Below: the silvery leaves of *Centaurea gymnocarpa* set off the daisy-like flowers of *Argyranthemum foeniculaceum*

Above: *Convolvulus mauritanicus* is ideal for a wide pot or a hanging basket and, although not hardy, is easily increased from cuttings

Below: *Cordyline australis*, sometimes known as cabbage tree, gives a distinctive accent to this mixed planting

flower. They must never be allowed to dry out. They benefit from regular feeding, preferably with a high potash fertilizer (such as a tomato fertilizer) which encourages flowering. (See also the Wisley handbook on camellias.)

CAMPANULA ISOPHYLLA

This trailing **bellflower** is a delightful addition to window boxes and hanging baskets and covers itself with starry blue or white blooms in summer. Sometimes seen as a houseplant, it is not hardy, but may be easily propagated from cuttings. (See p. 13.)

CANNA INDICA

This exotic-looking half-hardy perennial is grown both for foliage and for its showy pink, orange or red flowers. It requires a large container and can be raised from seed. During the winter the fleshy roots should be stored in frost-free conditions and subsequently divided for replanting in late spring.

CENTAUREA GYMNOCARPA

This shrubby plant with silver foliage is slightly tender but easily propagated from seed. Seed-raised plants can be rather coarse and variable in leaf colour. If you have a good form, it is worth keeping it going by taking cuttings in late summer. (See p. 32.)

CHEIRANTHUS

The brilliant orange flowers of the **Siberian wallflower**, *C. × allionii*, appear a little later than those of the ordinary wallflower. It is a shortlived perennial. Seed should be sown outside in midsummer for transplanting in the autumn, or on lighter soils in July and August to avoid premature flowering, the plants being thinned as necessary.

C. cheiri, the true **wallflower**, is still a favourite both for colour and scent. Generally speaking, plain rather than multicoloured kinds look better in a small container. Grown as a biennial, seed is sown outside in midsummer and transplanted into nursery rows, from where the plants are transferred to their flowering positions. Most cultivars grow to about 18 inches (50cm), but 'Orange Bedder' and the deep crimson 'Vulcan' are shorter. (See p. 45.)

34

CHRYSANTHEMUM

See *Argyranthemum*.

CINERARIA

See *Senecio*.

CLEMATIS

The 'queen of climbers' can look very effective grown in a large tub, either trained up wires or netting on a wall, or clambering over a tripod of canes fixed inside the container. (See p. 22.) The tub should be at least 1½ ft (45cm) deep and wide and plentiful watering and a weekly liquid feed will be necessary in the summer. A layer of pebbles on the surface of the compost helps to keep the roots cool. Spring- and early summer-flowering hybrids like the well-known 'Nelly Moser', 'Bees' Jubilee' and 'The President' are useful for north- or east-facing walls; autumn-flowering hybrids such as 'Comtesse de Bouchaud' and 'Jackmanii' prefer a sunny aspect. (See also the Wisley handbook on clematis.)

CONVOLVULUS

C. cneorum, although not entirely hardy, is a small shrub well worth growing for its silvery foliage and trumpet-shaped flowers of white tinged with pink, produced from late spring onwards. Cuttings taken in the summer will root readily in gentle heat.

The beautiful *C. mauritanicus* is slightly trailing and should be propagated by cuttings each autumn to ensure plants for the next summer (See p. 33.)

CORDYLINE

C. australis and *C. indivisa*, with the sword-like leaves held on a cylindrical stem, are equally impressive whether grown on their own in an urn or vase, or mixed with other plants for emphasis. They are hardy only in favoured areas and winter protection is necessary in most parts of the country. Propagation is from seed sown in warmth in March, which should result in a usable plant within about twelve months. (See p. 33.)

DATURA

See *Brugmansia*.

DIANTHUS

Carnations grown as annuals have become extremely popular and are excellent in containers. Sown in gentle heat in March and then pricked out into small pots or boxes, good-sized plants will come into bloom in June in their final containers and flower throughout the summer and autumn. Among the many forms available are 'Magic Charms' and 'Telstar', both of mixed colours; 'Snow Fire', which has single white flowers with scarlet centres; and the pretty, single-flowered 'Orchid'.

DIMORPHOTHECA

See *Osteospermum*.

DOROTHEANTHUS BELLIDIFORMIS

This tender annual succulent, often known as *Mesembryanthemum criniflorum*, has daisy-like flowers in a wide range of colours and should be grown in a container placed in full sun, without allowing the compost to dry out too much. Seed may be sown under glass in spring and the seedlings pricked out into boxes before being established in their flowering positions.

ELAEAGNUS

Two valuable variegated plants in this genus are *E.* × *ebbingei* 'Gilt Edge', with a gold band to the foliage, and *E. pungens* 'Maculata', which has leaves splashed with rich yellow. Both are large evergreen shrubs and should be grown in a spacious tub or barrel.

EUONYMUS FORTUNEI

'Emerald 'n' Gold' and 'Emerald Gaiety', gold- and silver-variegated respectively, are two excellent hardy evergreen shrubs. They may be allowed to trail or climb and will do equally well in sun or shade. 'Kewensis' is a miniature version with plain green leaves. All can be easily increased from cuttings at almost any time of year.

FATSIA JAPONICA

A familiar house plant, this imposing evergreen is a splendid specimen shrub for an outside container. Its glossy palmate leaves are complemented by white flowers in the autumn and it is perfectly hardy. It may be increased by cuttings taken in late summer. It is very useful for a shady situation.

FELICIA AMELLOIDES

This half-hardy perennial may be propagated by cuttings in autumn or spring. In growth it tends to cascade and bears bright blue daisy-like flowers which continue all summer. There is also a variegated form.

FUCHSIA

These well-known summer-flowering shrubs are grown in all sorts of containers and the pendulous forms are particularly suitable for hanging baskets. There are many cultivars to choose from, including some with variegated or golden foliage. It is important that the plants are kept well-watered and fed during the growing season. During the dormant winter period they should be protected from frost. Softwood cuttings root very readily in the spring. (See also the Wisley handbook on fuchsias.)

Recommended trailing or semi-trailing types include 'Auntie Jinks'; 'Bon Bon'; 'Bouffant'; 'Cascade'; 'Daisy Bell'; 'Golden Marinka' with golden foliage; 'Marinka'; 'Red Spider'; 'Summer Snow'; and 'White Spider'.

Among the bush forms are the compact 'Alice Hoffman'; 'Army Nurse'; 'Charming'; 'Golden Treasure'; 'Levorkusen'; 'Sunray', with variegated leaves; and the dwarf 'Tom Thumb'.

The free-flowering *Fuchsia* 'Thalia' and a zonal pelargonium

A modern container makes a bold display with petunias and the
feathery rich green leaves of *Grevillea robusta*

GAZANIA

Grown as a half-hardy annual, this member of the daisy family
revels in full sun and to a certain extent withstands dry conditions. Selected forms can only be propagated from cuttings,
taken in autumn and spring, although it is more usually raised
from seed. Recent strains include Sundance, in shades of scarlet,
orange, carmine pink and bronze, and Ministar, yellow and white.

GLECHOMA HEDERACEA 'VARIEGATA'

The variegated **ground ivy**, with white-splashed leaves and long
trailing stems, is a good plant for hanging baskets. It is a hardy
perennial and should be propagated from cuttings under glass in
spring.

GREVILLEA ROBUSTA

This is a perfect accent plant, its decorative ferny leaves provid-
ing a wonderful foil for most other plants grown with it. It is a
tender shrub and can be difficult to raise from seed. However,
plants propagated in the summer will be about 2 feet (60cm) high
the following spring.

HEDERA HELIX

The common **ivy** and its many forms are invaluable in hanging baskets and, because of their hardiness, can even be left outside in winter. They may be trained into a pyramid or fan or simply allowed to trail over the edge. They need to be trimmed in the spring to keep them tidy. Variegated ivies look particularly well in shady situations and are useful in problem areas such as a north-facing wall or patio. They are readily increased from semi-hardwood cuttings at almost any time of year. (See pp. 40 and 59.)

HEBE

Generally neat and compact in habit, the shrubby **veronicas** produce their panicles of bloom in shades of white, lavender or pink from spring to autumn. They are evergreen and easily grown, although they may suffer in severe winters. Propagation is from cuttings of young wood in the summer. There are numerous garden hybrids available as well as the species.

HELICHRYSUM

H. microphyllum is a small-leaved, silver-grey foliage plant. It is not too rampant and is good for edging or filling a container. Cuttings should be rooted in spring or autumn.

H. petiolare is a much coarser sprawling shrub, with woolly grey leaves. It is often seen as a bedding plant but is excellent in larger containers and hanging baskets. It should be overwintered in a frost-free place. A variegated form is obtainable and also a yellow-leaved sort, 'Sulphureum', sometimes known wrongly as 'Limelight'. Cuttings should be rooted in spring or autumn, as an insurance against loss of the parent plant.

HYDRANGEA

Hortensia and lacecap hydrangeas are often grown in tubs or barrels and their flowers make a welcome contribution in late summer and autumn. There are many other excellent hydrangeas for the purpose, such as the distinctive 'Ayesha', with its lilac-like blooms; *H. paniculata*, with creamy white pyramidal panicles, and its forms 'Grandiflora' and 'Praecox'; and the smaller *H. serrata* 'Grayswood' and 'Preziosa'. All hydrangeas need large containers and should never be allowed to dry out. It is wise to give them some protection in severe winters. Old flowering wood

Above: a hortensia hydrangea with ivy in a terracotta pot—a good combination of two reliable plants for permanent containers

Below: *Ipomoea* 'Flying Saucers' left to scramble around a window box

on hortensias and lacecaps should be removed annually for best effect, while *H. paniculata* requires pruning each spring to one or two pairs of buds from the previous year's growth.

IMPATIENS

Busy lizzies have become extremely popular over the last decade or so and plant breeders are producing numerous cultivars, some with double flowers. They thrive in cool shade and in sun, flowering continuously throughout the summer and autumn until the frosts. Though perennial, they are usually treated as a half-hardy annual. Seed should be germinated at a minimum temperature of 70°F (21°C), in full light and high humidity, enclosing the seed tray in a polythene bag. (See pp. 6, 10 and 18.)

IPOMOEA

The **morning glories** are mostly climbers for training up a trellis in a sunny position. However, the small-growing cultivar 'Minibar Rose' can be encouraged to trail. Its leaves resemble those of a variegated ivy and it bears a profusion of trumpet-shaped flowers, rose-pink edged with white. Germination can be assisted by chipping the seeds (nicking or scratching the hard outer coat) or soaking them in warm water overnight before sowing. It is definitely a half-hardy annual.

LANTANA

In the past it was quite easy to buy seed of *L. camara*, a half-hardy shrub, but it is now stocked by only a very few firms. However, rooted cuttings or established plants of selected colour forms are sometimes available from local nurseries. Although prone to whitefly infestation, it makes an excellent semi-trailing container plants, with dense flowerheads ranging in colour from white, pink, lilac and mauve to orange and red.

L. selloviana is a rosy lilac species which is much more slender in growth but equally decorative.

LATHYRUS

The **sweet pea**, a climbing hardy annual, is a universal favourite. Tall-growing sweet peas are available in a whole range of different shades and do particularly well in growing bags, although troughs, tubs and other containers are quite adequate.

41

Some support should be provided in the form of string, netting, canes or twiggy sticks. However, the dwarf cultivars, which reach about 3 feet (1m) in height, are less likely to need staking or can simply be allowed to cascade. They are good in vases or urns and come in mixed colours, for instance Knee Hi and Jet Set. Seed should be sown in early spring in gentle heat.

LAURUS NOBILIS

The sweet **bay tree**, clipped into a round or oval outline, is the archetypal container plant. It should be pruned to shape during the growing season. Although it is hardy, the foliage tends to be damaged by wind or frost scorch and it should have some winter protection.

LAVANDULA

Among the **lavenders**, the popular 'Hidcote' and the so-called Dutch lavender L. *vera*, as it is wrongly known, are especially recommended. The first is a compact silvery shrub with dense spikes of violet flowers appearing in early July. The second is somewhat taller and later flowering.

LEUCOPHYTA

See *Calocephalus*.

LILIUM

Some of the most reliable **lilies** for growing in pots and tubs are L. *auratum*, L. *longiflorum*, L. *speciosum*, L. *lancifolium* (L. *tigrinum*) and the hybrid 'Enchantment'. They need fairly deep containers and a well-drained compost and may be planted individually in 6 to $7\frac{1}{2}$ inch (15–20cm) pots or several together in a larger tub. The bulbs should be potted in spring and stood in a cold frame or in the shelter of a wall or hedge. It is advisable to cover the surface with a layer of peat or leaf mould and to give little or no water until the roots have developed and the shoots are emerging. The pots may then be moved to their summer positions, in sun or light shade. (See also the Wisley handbook on lilies.)

LOBELIA

The trailing lobelia, L. *erinus*, is an ever-popular hanging basket plant, with many cultivars available including 'Light Blue Basket',

Blue lobelia is one of the most worthwhile plants for hanging baskets

'Blue Basket' and 'Red Cascade'. The compact edging types can be used to good effect in other containers. In this category 'Cambridge Blue' and 'Crystal Palace', with dark foliage and deep blue flowers, and 'Rosamond', crimson-flowered with a white eye, are all satisfactory. A half-hardy perennial generally grown as an annual, it is propagated by seed sown in gentle heat during February and March.

L. valida is a much stronger growing species than *L. erinus* and may be raised from seed or cuttings. Its clear blue flowers with a distinct white centre blend particularly well with other plants and it deserves to be more widely grown.

LOBULARIA MARITIMA

Sweet alyssum is a well-known edger and, although a true hardy annual, it is better raised as a half-hardy, sown under glass in late March to April. As well as the familiar white forms like 'Snowdrift' and 'Carpet of Snow', there are several attractive coloured forms, such as the rich purple 'Oriental Night', lilac pink 'Rosie O' Day', purple 'Royal Carpet' and red purple 'Wonderland'.

MESEMBRYANTHEMUM

See *Dorotheanthus*.

MIMULUS MOSCHATUS

With recent developments in plant breeding, there are now a number of F_1 hybrids on the market, including 'Royal Velvet', mahogany red with a spotted golden throat; 'Malibu Orange'; and 'Calipso Mixed'. The **musk** is a hardy perennial and should be kept well watered, which will ensure a long flowering season. Seed is sown under glass in early spring.

MYOSOTIS SYLVATICA

The biennial **forget-me-not** is an old favourite for spring flowers. Seed should be sown outside in the summer and the plants grown on in nursery rows before transferring to their final positions in containers. 'Blue Ball', 'Blue Banquet' and 'Royal Blue' are the best among the various shades of blue. 'Carmine King' and 'Rose Pink' are examples of other colours and there is also a white form, although it is not outstanding.

Above: a well known but charming combination of forget-me-nots and dwarf wallflowers in a half-barrel

Below: nicotiana Nicki Mixture and lobelia make a fine display in a permanent brick container

NEMESIA STRUMOSA

This brightly coloured half-hardy annual is an ideal plant for containers. Seeds should be sown in heat in March and the seedlings pricked out into boxes for hardening off, before planting when the risk of frosts has passed. Carnival Mixture is the best for general purposes, bearing large flowers on compact plants, while 'Blue Gem' is more slender in growth and intermingles well.

NICOTIANA AFFINIS

The **tobacco plant**, with its scented white flowers, grows to a height of about 3 feet (1m) and is therefore only suitable for large containers. However, hybridists have made great advances, resulting in short compact plants with upward-facing flowers which open in the day. Unfortunately, the perfume has been diminished in the process, except in the taller forms like 'Evening Fragrance', coming in a mixture of pink, red, mauve, purple and white. 'Domino Mixed' grows to one foot (30cm) high and Nicki Mixture to only 10 inches (25cm), both covering a good range of colours including lime green. Seed of this half-hardy annual may be sown under glass as late as April. (See p. 45.)

OSTEOSPERMUM

This group of daisy-like annuals and perennials includes *Dimorphotheca*, which is the more usual name for those annuals raised from seed, such as *D. aurantiaca* 'Glistening White' and 'Giant Orange'.

Of the perennial *Osteospermum* there are some excellent named cultivars, including 'Blue Streak', white and blue; 'Buttermilk', yellow; 'Tresco Purple', purple, low-growing; 'Whirligig', white, with spoon-shaped petals showing the reverse side of blue. All these are half-hardy and require full sun to perform well. They are best overwintered as young plants raised from cuttings, which should be taken in late summer.

PELARGONIUM

The **geraniums**, as they are commonly known, need no introduction. They revel in sunny positions and, although they can withstand a certain amount of dryness, they need to be kept properly watered and fed to give of their best.

The ivy-leaved geraniums, with their slender stems and tendency to trail, are perfect in hanging baskets and for edging window boxes and other containers. (See p. 13.) Recommended cultivars are 'Ailsa Garland', deep pink; 'Blue Spring', with shorter trailing growths and mauve-purple flowers; 'Crocodile', pink with cream-netted variegation; 'Galilee', rose-pink; 'Mme Crousse', pale pink; 'Rouletta', white flowers with red streaks; 'Scarlet Crousse'; 'Snowdrift'; 'Tania' and 'Yale', light and deep crimson; and 'White Mesh', gold-netted variegation on the leaves and rose-pink flowers. Some very profuse-flowering kinds have been introduced recently from the Continent and are becoming more widely available.

The traditional zonal pelargoniums are equally at home in a variety of containers and, like the ivy-leaved ones, flower through-out the summer and on into early autumn. Among the single-flowered kinds are the orange-red 'Maxim Kovaleski' and scarlet 'Paul Crampel'. Double-flowered cultivars include 'A.A. Mayne', magenta; 'Double Henry Jacoby', bright red; 'Gustav Emich', scarlet; 'Hermine', white; 'King of Denmark', salmon-pink; 'Mrs Lawrence', clear pink; 'Orangesonne', brilliant orange; and 'Ted Brook', purple. Zonals that may be raised from seed are 'Cherry Diamond', vivid red; 'Hollywood Star', rose-pink and white; 'Orbit White'; and 'Scarlet Diamond'. (See pp. 15 and 37.)

Variegated and coloured-leaf geraniums are very attractive, although the flowers may be relatively insignificant. A selection of cultivars is 'Caroline Schmidt', silver with bright red double flowers; 'Chelsea Gem', silver and pink; 'Crystal Palace Gem', yellow leaves with green markings and rose flowers; 'Dolly Varden', tricolor foliage of cream, rosy red and green with red flowers; 'Flower of Spring', silver with single scarlet flowers; 'Frank Headley', small silver leaves and salmon flowers; 'Golden Harry Hieover', with a chestnut zone on golden green leaves and red flowers; 'Happy Thought', yellow butterfly patches on bright green with rose flowers; 'Lady Plymouth', cream and green varie-gation; 'Mrs Parker', silver and rose-pink; 'Mrs Pollock', golden tricolor with orange-red flowers; and 'Mrs Quilter', bronze and pink.

Over the past decade, hybridists have made great progress in developing seed-raised strains of the zonal pelargoniums and even the ivy-leaved geranium is now receiving their attention. Seed can be sown in autumn or spring, when a temperature of 74°F (23°C) should be maintained to ensure good germination.

Ideally the seedlings should be grown on in a temperature of 60° to 65°F (16°–18°C). However, many gardeners still prefer to propagate from cuttings as it can be expensive to provide the necessary warmth to bring young seed-raised plants through the winter. (See also the Wisley handbook on pelargoniums.)

PERILLA FRUTESCENS

This is a fine purple-leaved plant attaining about 2 feet (60cm) in height, which is best used as an accent plant in larger containers. The forms *nankinensis* and *laciniata* are very ornamental with their curly-edged and deeply cut leaves. It is a half-hardy annual, raised from seed sown under glass in the spring. The flowers are relatively insignificant.

A splendid mass of petunias concealing the container

PETUNIA

Deservedly popular for all sorts of containers, petunia cultivars are available in a quite bewildering number. They range in height and also in colour, through white, yellow, pink, red, blue and purple, together with striped and bicolors. Recent introductions include strains which are less susceptible to damage from rain. Seed of this half-hardy annual is sown in gentle heat under glass in spring and should be left uncovered to ensure good germination. (See also p. 38.)

PHORMIUM TENAX

This is an exotic evergreen foliage plant with long sword-like leaves, suitable for a large container. Some of the more recently introduced types with striking variegation are of doubtful hardiness, but all are tolerant of a wide range of conditions.

POLYGONUM CAPITATUM

This half-hardy perennial is a good trailing plant for hanging baskets and other containers in a sheltered spot. The zoned evergreen leaves and small pink globular heads of flower remain attractive throughout the growing season. Seed should be sown in March under glass.

PORTULACA

Grown as a half-hardy annual, this makes a nice edging plant for a small container in full sun, with richly coloured flowers of rose, orange, rosy purple, yellow or white. The double forms, although expensive, are the most easily obtainable and of these 'Sunglo' is by far the best. Seed should be sown under glass in March.

PRIMULA

The **polyanthus** is the most useful representative of this large genus for growing in a container and one of the finest of all the spring-flowering plants. There are many good strains available. Seed may be sown in heat under glass in January or February or in a cold frame in April or May. The seedlings should be pricked off into boxes and subsequently planted in nursery rows, before moving to their flowering positions in containers. After flowering the best plants can be retained by lifting them, splitting down to single crowns and planting in a reserve bed. (See p. 16.)

Rhododendron 'Madam Masson', perfect for brightening the corner of a terrace or a similar shady spot

RHODODENDRON

Most rhododendrons are potential container plants, given a large enough tub. Gardeners with chalky or limy soil, where rhododendrons rarely succeed, will also find this a useful method. Rhododendrons require a lime-free compost (for instance, Arthur Bower's ericaceous) and plentiful watering. The beautiful hybrids of the dwarf *R. yakushimanum*, producing their abundant flowers in a range of colours in May and June, are particularly worthwhile. (See also the Wisley handbook on rhododendrons.)

RICINUS COMMUNIS

The true **castor oil plant** is an elegant tropical shrub, usually treated as a half-hardy annual. The bold palmate leaves and conspicuous spiny fruits are very impressive in a large mixed display of plants or when several are grouped alone in a single container. Two forms, 'Gibsonii' and 'Impala', have bronze-red leaves, the latter with particularly striking flowers and fruits. The variety *zanzibarensis* has very large, bright green, veined leaves up to 2 feet (60cm) across. They are readily raised from seed sown under glass in spring.

SALPIGLOSSIS SINUATA

This is one of the most beautiful half-hardy annuals, with large trumpet-shaped flowers in various colours and often patterned or striped. 'Bolero' and 'Flash' are two very good recent introductions. From a spring sowing under glass, plants will grow to about 2 feet (60cm). However, much stronger specimens will result from an autumn sowing, needing just frost-free conditions to keep them going through the winter, and will flower in May and June.

SALVIA

The common **sage**, *S. officinalis*, with its felted grey aromatic leaves, has been cultivated as a herb for centuries. It is also an ideal small hardy shrub for containers, particularly in the variegated version, 'Icterina', and the purple-leaved form, 'Purpurascens'. It is readily increased from cuttings in the sumer.

Generally grown as a half-hardy annual, *S. farinacea* is a fairly vigorous plant and can be useful for its upright habit. The cultivar 'Victoria' carries dense spikes of violet blue flowers. Seed sown in March under glass will result in plants ready for planting out in the south by the beginning of June.

There is probably no better red flowering plant for summer display than the familiar *S. splendens*. Among a number of cultivars, 'Carabinière', 'Red Hussar', 'Red Silver' and 'Royal Mountie' can be recommended. Seed sown in early spring requires temperatures of 68°F (18°C) to germinate freely and reasonable warmth afterwards to get the plants growing away strongly. Although it is preferable to raise them singly in pots, plants can be successful in trays so long as the roots do not

51

become too box-bound. Rose, pink, purple and white forms can also be found, though usually in seedsmen's mixtures.

SEDUM SPECTABILE

This autumn-flowering perennial succulent is perfect for a hot, dry situation. Although it will, of course, require watering in a container, it can survive periods of drought without ill effect. The cool green foliage is handsome throughout the summer, followed by flat flowerheads of pink which attract butterflies. 'Autumn Joy' has bright rose flowers and purplish stems, while 'Brilliant', with bright pink flowers, is one of the best of the **ice plants**.

SENECIO CINERARIA

Often listed as *Cineraria maritima*, this neat silver-grey shrub is half-hardy and should be raised from seed sown under glass.

STENOTAPHRUM SECUNDATUM 'VARIEGATUM'

This tropical creeping ornamental grass with cream-striped leaves is attractive in hanging baskets. It is easily propagated from cuttings at any time.

TAGETES

This generic name embraces the **African** and **French marigolds** and hybrids of the two. Many cultivars have been raised with single, double or crested-centre flowers, in shades of yellow to orange, and ranging in height from 6 to 15 inches (15–38cm). They are all invaluable in containers, making a fine display over a long period, and are easy to germinate under glass in spring for growing on and then planting out after the frosts. (See p. 15.)

T. tenuifolia pumila, another half-hardy annual, forms bushy plants which are profusely covered in single flowers. It grows up to 10 inches (25cm) high, depending on the cultivar, and is equally easy to raise from seed.

THUNBERGIA ALATA

Black-eyed Susan is a climbing or trailing plant to approximately 3 feet (1m) high. It has white, yellow or orange flowers, usually with a black centre, although the cultivar 'Susie' lacks the dark

Thunbergia alata trained into a spectacular column

eye. Grown as a half-hardy annual, it is raised from seed sown under glass in April.

TOLMIEA MENZIESII

Sometimes seen as a house plant, this evergreen perennial is completely hardy and very adaptable, thriving outside in a semi-shaded position. It may be planted on its own in a hanging basket and, although not fully trailing, will soon cover it with heart-shaped leaves, green or variegated. Propagation is by division in autumn to spring or alternatively, in late summer and autumn, by pegging down individual leaves which will form small plantlets at the base—whence the common name pig-a-back plant.

TROPAEOLUM

The gardener's **nasturtium**, *T. majus*, is perfect for pots, baskets and window boxes, although unfortunately prone to attack by blackfly. Double Gleam Hybrids can be recommended for general use and grow to about 15 inches (38cm). 'Alaska' is an interesting cultivar with variegated foliage about one foot (30cm) high, while 'Jewel Mixed' and the dark-leaved, crimson-flowered 'Empress of India' are even dwarfer. All nasturtiums can be sown *in situ* or grown singly in smaller pots for subsequent planting out in containers. A sunny position is important for them to flower well.

T. peregrinum, the **canary creeper**, is a vigorous climber which bears abundant small lemon-yellow flowers in summer. Seed should be sown in April under glass.

VERBENA

Several mixed strains of *V. × hybrida* are on the market, together with single coloured forms in pink, scarlet and violet blue. These are all grown as half-hardy annuals and raised from seed, which at times can prove difficult. Keeping the compost fairly dry will encourage even germination and temperatures of 68° to 78°F (20°–25°C) are recommended. In addition, some excellent named kinds have been selected, which must be propagated by cuttings taken in autumn and spring and require protection from frost in winter. They include 'Lawrence Johnston', crimson; 'Loveliness', mauve-violet; 'Silver Ann' also known as 'Pink Bouquet', strong pink; and 'Sissinghurst', magenta.

Three perennial verbenas are worthy of note. *V. rigida* (*V. venosa*), with purple flowers, is a somewhat stiff plant reaching a height of about 2 feet (60cm), and *V. canadensis* (*V. aubletia* of catalogues) has magenta flowers. Both come fairly readily from spring-sown seed. Grown as a half-hardy annual, *V. peruviana* (*V. chamaedrifolia* or *V. chamaedrioides*) is of slender habit, with bright red flowers, and is propagated from cuttings. *V. tenera* 'Mahonettii' is reddish violet with the petals rayed and margined white. It is a slightly weak-growing plant, which needs care in overwintering, and should be propagated by cuttings.

VINCA

The **periwinkles**, *V. major* and *V. minor*, are vigorous trailers which do well in sun or shade. There are several decorative varie-

Above: the unusual variegated nasturtium 'Alaska', with its flowers of many colours, may be grown in a hanging basket or simply allowed to sprawl

Below: verbena 'Loveliness' mixed with *Felicia amelloides*, helichrysum and centaurea

gated forms and the flowers, usually bright blue, are borne continuously throughout the spring and early summer. They are very easy to propagate from cuttings.

VIOLA

Pansies are invaluable container plants and there have been great advances in breeding, especially with the winter-flowering types. These will flower continuously from the autumn through to spring, depending on the weather, and are ideal not only in pots and window boxes but also in hanging baskets. They are easily raised from seed sown in June or July in trays or prepared beds and then pricked out into boxes or nursery rows. 'Azure Blue', Universal Mixture and Golden Champion are good choices.

Summer-flowering pansies are particularly useful for containers in shaded positions. They include 'Ullswater'; 'Crimson Queen'; Clear Crystals Mixed; and Roggli Giant. They are usually grown as half-hardy annuals, from seed sown in early spring. (See pp. 18 and 60.)

ZEA MAYS

The variegated **sweetcorn**, with its white- or yellow-and-white striped leaves, is an imposing plant which remains decorative throughout the growing season. It is an annual, easily raised from seed and grown on singly in pots, and will require a fairly large container.

ZINNIA ELEGANS

This half-hardy annual can be obtained in a very wide range of colour, size and shape of flower. The giant-flowered kinds may attain 2 feet (60cm) or more, some having quilled petals, others giving a ruffled effect. There are also many fully double and single-flowered sorts, with both large and small blooms. The shorter ones, growing 6 to 12 inches (15–30cm) high, make excellent edgers. The young plants resent root disturbance and are best grown on from seedlings in small pots, having been sown in March and germinated at 68°F (20°C). They flower particularly well in hot dry summers.

A trough garden planted with saxifrage and sempervivum, two of the easiest alpines

ALPINES

There are many exquisite gems among the alpines that lend themselves to container growing. One of their main attractions is that such a large number of different species can be grown in a small space and, with careful choice, a permanent miniature garden can be created. Old or simulated stone troughs are ideal, most requiring an open, sunny situation and very sharp drainage. The list below is just a small sample of the many plants suitable for sinks and troughs. (See also the Wisley handbook on alpines.)

Alyssum serpyllifolia—a dense grey mat of leaves with bright yellow flowers in June.

Aquilegia bertolonii—tufts of hairy greyish green foliage and violet-blue columbine flowers in May.

Artemisia assoanum—a prostrate spreading foliage plant with silver leaves.

Asperula caespitosa lilaciflora—a carpet of bright green leaves with tubular, deep carmine blooms in summer.

Campanula arvatica 'Alba'—large white starry flowers borne above bright green leaves in June.

Cyananthus microphyllus—a trailing plant related to campanula, with blue flowers in August; best in a shady position.

Dianthus alpinus—cushion-forming, with fringed carnation flowers of pink and white in June.

Draba aizoides—a hummock of small rigid leaves covered in pale yellow flowers in April.

Dryas octopetala 'Minor'—a creeper with woolly leaves and white flowers followed by fluffy seedheads.

Gentiana verna angulosa—a form of the well-known spring gentian, producing rich blue flowers in April.

Helianthemum alpestre 'Serpyllifolium'—a prostrate rock rose with abundant yellow saucer-shaped flowers in summer.

Ilex crenata 'Mariesii'—a slow-growing dwarf holly.

Juniperus communis 'Compressa'—a miniature juniper of columnar habit and dense grey-green foliage.

Phlox douglasii 'Crackerjack'—a thick mat with a profusion of crimson-red flowers in early summer.

Potentilla nitida 'Rubra'—large deep rose-pink flowers in July and August above ground-hugging silvery leaves.

Primula marginata forms—easily grown alpines valued for their mealy leaves and delightful scented flowers in various shades of lavender.

Ramonda myconi —a rosette of green leaves and large open flowers of pale blue with yellow centres in early summer; prefers a shady spot.

Salix × *boydii*—a beautiful dwarf willow with pale yellow catkins in May.

Saxifraga—plants in the Euaizoonia section form rosettes of silvery leaves and bear elegant starry flowers in summer; those in the Engleria and Kabschia sections are smaller and denser, with saucer-shaped blooms; *S. oppositifolia* 'Ruth Draper' is creeping and has cup-shaped flowers of rich red in spring.

Sedum cauticolum—a trailing mat with grey-green leaves and deep purple-red flowers in September.

Sempervivum—the houseleeks, with succulent evergreen leaves in tight rosettes; the cobweb houseleek, *S. arachnoideum*, has the added attraction of bright rose-red flowers in summer and 'Minor' is a choice form.

Sisyrinchium macounianum 'Album'—fans of small leaves like an iris and numerous large white flowers.

Sorbus reducta—a diminutive slow-growing shrub with crimson berries and fine autumn foliage.

BULBS

Spring-flowering bulbs are always welcome for their cheerful colours early in the year and, in many respects, are ideal for containers. They are easily grown, require little attention, except for occasional watering to prevent the compost drying out, and succeed in sun or shade and in a sheltered or exposed position.

However, bulbs have two obvious disadvantages. After planting in the autumn, they do not produce results for several months and the containers remain bare during this time; and, once they have flowered, the leaves start to die down and the plants become untidy. A solution to both these problems is to grow the bulbs in pots and transfer them to the container as they come into bloom, replacing as necessary those which are already over. Alternatively, bulbs can simply be treated as bedding plants, to be planted, enjoyed and then discarded.

Dwarf bulbs are the most practical and rewarding choice for containers and it is wiser to avoid tall-growing daffodils and tulips, as they tend to be damaged by the wind. For maximum effect, the bulbs should be planted in generous groups, rather than regimented rows, and close together (no more than an inch apart).

Mixed daffodils and ivy in a decorative old container

Dwarf tulips edged with pansies and nicely in scale with the urn

They can also be planted in layers, burying the larger bulbs deep in the compost and interspersing the smaller ones above them nearer the surface. However, containers often look better if devoted to a single kind of bulb, which ensures that all flower together to produce a bold display.

Bulbs are particularly attractive in window boxes, where they can be appreciated close at hand. They can, of course, be grown in special bulb pots and bowls or planted around the base of trees and shrubs in large tubs. Some of the daintier types, which might otherwise be too inconspicuous, can be given a permanent home in a sink or trough, mingled with alpines. These might include snowdrops, winter aconites and anemones like *A. blanda*, which can be slow to establish and are therefore unsuitable for a seasonal window box. Miniature daffodils, irises, chionodoxas, crocuses, cyclamen and fritillaries can be used too, so long as their foliage remains fairly neat after flowering and does not spoil the overall appearance of the sink garden.

For window boxes and similar containers, there is a wide range of dwarf bulbs. The yellow *Iris danfordiae* is valuable for its very early flowering, followed by the blue *Iris reticulata* in March and April. *Crocus chrysanthus* and its cultivars also bloom in February, although the later Dutch crocuses are perhaps more striking with their large flowers. Grape hyacinths and scillas are both very easy to grow and are most decorative interplanted with other bulbs or polyanthus and winter-flowering pansies.

Among the daffodils, the hybrids of *Narcissus cyclamineus* such as 'Peeping Tom' and 'February Gold' and the increasingly popular 'Tête-à-Tête' grow no more than about 9 inches (23cm) high and make a delightful contribution early in the year. The species itself is excellent in a sink or trough, as is *N. bulbocodium*, the hoop petticoat daffodil. Some of the Triandrus daffodils, with two to three blooms per stem, and the scented jonquils are under 12 inches (30cm) in height and 'W. P. Milner' is a dwarf white trumpet daffodil.

With their large flowers in brilliant colours and sturdy stems, the shorter-growing tulips are especially useful in containers. The species *Tulipa fosteriana*, *T. greigii* and *T. kaufmanniana* and their hybrids can all be recommended and together flower from March to May. Single early and double early tulips, blooming in April, are also widely available.

CONIFERS

There is quite a selection of dwarf conifers worth considering as permanent plants for troughs and tubs. Together with alpines they can be used to create a delightful miniature garden. Larger-growing specimens may be grown singly in bigger containers but will need generous watering and regular feeding during the growing season.

The many forms of the false cypress, *Chamaecyparis lawsoniana*, are all recommended for container planting, particularly 'Brunhill Gold'; 'Ellwoodii', initially fast-growing and then becoming more sedate; and 'Minima Glauca' and the golden 'Minima Aurea', both bun-shaped. 'Krippsii', 'Nana Gracilis' and 'Pygmaea' are good dwarf cultivars of *C. obtusa* and the popular *C. pisifera* 'Boulevard' is a dense bush of medium size.

Another great favourite is *Crypotomeria japonica* 'Vilmoriniana', which is a tight small globe and very slow growing.

The junipers are useful for sunny positions and the prostrate and spreading kinds contrast well with upright growing plants. Again they will be best in very large containers. Some recommended cultivars are *J. chinensis* 'Blaauw's Variety', cylindrical in

Half-barrels planted with conifers and crocus

habit and blue-grey in leaf; *J. communis* 'Compressa', conical and tight-growing; *J.* × *media* 'Pfitzeriana' and 'Pfitzeriana Aurea', both fairly wide-spreading; *J. squamata* 'Blue Carpet', which is aptly named, and 'Blue Star'; and *J.* 'Grey Owl', spreading to 5 feet (1.5m) or more. (See also the Wisley handbook on dwarf and slow-growing conifers.)

VEGETABLES

Vegetables of all kinds can be grown in containers—growing bags, large pots and tubs, even window boxes—although crops will obviously be fairly limited. Containers are also extremely useful for obtaining earlier results in a heated or cool greenhouse, especially with potatoes, spring onions, peas (Early Onward, Meteor) and dwarf broad beans (The Sutton).

Runner and dwarf French beans, beetroot, stump-rooted carrots, courgettes, tomatoes, radishes, cucumbers and lettuce are all suitable for growing bags.

HERBS

Herbs are ideal for growing bags, pots, window boxes, and of

Above: aubergines will thrive in a growing bag and can look very ornamental

Below: the familiar but still unbeatable association of geraniums with silvery helichrysum and cineraria

course, special herb containers. They are rarely needed in large quantities and they look decorative at the same time. They can also be moved indoors to ensure a fresh supply throughout the year.

FRUIT

Grapes, peaches and figs lend themselves readily to cultivation in large pots and tubs. Some sort of protection from frost is desirable, either hessian or bracken or a cold greenhouse, but they will succeed in a sheltered sunny position on a patio. Reliable varieties of grape are 'Black Hamburgh' and 'Foster's Seedling', both early-fruiting; of peach 'Peregrine' and 'Rochester'; and of fig 'Brown Turkey'. (See also the Wisley handbook on grapes and *The Fruit Garden Displayed*.)

Dessert apples on very dwarf root stocks (M.9 and M.27) can also be grown in large containers.

Strawberries are excellent container plants for tubs, special strawberry pots and growing bags. In the latter case, they can be planted as a second crop to follow lettuces or cucumbers.

M